YOUR
POCKET
THERAPIST

WHEN YOU'RE LIVING
WITH A TROUBLED TEEN

Restoring Peace in the Home

Dr. David B. Hawkins, ACSW, Ph.D.

"Don't laugh at a youth for his affectations; he is only trying on one face after another to find his own."

—LOGAN PEARSALL SMITH

Victor is an imprint of
Cook Communications Ministries, Colorado Springs, Colorado 80918
Cook Communications, Paris, Ontario
Kingsway Communications, Eastbourne, England

WHEN YOU'RE LIVING WITH A TROUBLED TEEN
© 2001 by David B. Hawkins

ISBN: 0-78143-737-7
First Printing, 2001
Printed in the United States of America

Editors: Craig Bubeck, John Conaway
Cover & Interior Design: Global Images and iDesignEtc.

About the Author

A licensed clinical psychologist trained in the fields of social work and clinical psychology, Dr. David B. Hawkins, ACSW, Ph.D., has been in private practice for more than twenty years and specializes in domestic violence, adult and family issues, and marriage enrichment. Based in Longview, Washington, he is a certified domestic violence perpetrator treatment provider, certified forensic examiner, and a spiritual director. He also is a member of the National Association of Social Workers, Academy of Forensic Examiners, and the American Psychological Association. The author of several other books, including *See Dick and Jane Grow Up* (ISBN: 0-78143-498-X), David

has co-hosted a weekly radio broadcast entitled "Right Where You Live," was the host of an award-winning television program entitled "Community Forum," and writes a monthly column for the *Longview Daily News* entitled "Matters of the Heart."

INTRODUCTION

A former pastor calls our home. Our families have known each other for years. We have watched our children grow from adorable infants, to awkward middle-schoolers, to teenagers with attitudes. He and his wife are extremely distraught this evening because their daughter has seemingly changed overnight. Once a delightful innocent girl in pigtails, now she demands several earrings in her ears and one in her navel as well.

Our friends feel like they're being held captive. Just a short time ago they struggled with decisions about their daughter's well-being, but there was never any doubt about who had the authority in their home. Now everything is a debate. Not only is there debate about earrings and body-piercing, but appropriate clothing has also become an issue. Curfews are hotly debated, as are choice of friends. Each day brings a new power struggle, along with heartache, distance, and fiery tempers. The pastor asks me what he has done wrong.

Another friend, whose son has been picked up several times for alcohol abuse, shares his confusion. While none of the problems are earth-shattering in their own right, the cumulative effect upon him and his wife is debilitating. They painfully watch their son turn from someone they know and love to someone they struggle to like. Their son has had troubles with the law and is rebelling from all the values that he has been painstakingly taught. They never dreamed *they* would have a prodigal son. That only happened to other families.

The headlines of the local newspaper echoed what had been screaming across the airwaves the entire day. There had been another adolescent spraying bullets into a crowded schoolroom for no apparent reason. Some innocent children were killed; many were wounded. The nation's attention was riveted to the unfolding events. The debriefing of the well-trained staff at the school indicated that a disgruntled adolescent had been bullied and decided to take revenge into his own hands. He had been hurting for months, and now decided to hurt others.

There has been a flurry of calls to my office in recent years by extremely distressed parents of adolescents. Many of these parents feel ill-equipped to deal with the turbulence that often occurs with teenagers. While they were raising their families, they became used to having the power to influence their child's behavior, but during the teen years they find their power and control waning. In some situations this can be handled as a minor adjustment in family functioning, while in others it creates a house divided. **Your Pocket Therapist** will look at ways to reunite the divided home.

A TIME OF CHANGE

To say that adolescence is a time of change is an understatement. It tends to be an extremely tumultuous time not only for the youth, but for the entire family. When one person changes in a family, all are affected. These changes cause an upheaval in family functioning. What is so disconcerting is that many families are unprepared to face this onslaught of emotionality, willpower, and apparent rebellion. It is a time of confusion.

What can we say to the family whose delightful daughter suddenly begins swearing at them and violating sacred family rules? How do we understand the sudden Jekyl-and-Hyde changes in personality? They can be happy and charming one moment—angry, manipulative, and sullen the next. The family can feel like they are on one long roller-coaster ride. But this ride is no fun. Where and when will it end? **Your Pocket Therapist** will help answer some of these questions.

Fortunately, in all of this chaos we can find glimmers of hope. You may be desperate for a dose of hope right now. There are several encouraging signs on the horizon. Here are some positive facts for you to think about.

First, these changes are normal and to be expected. God designed us to go through developmental changes *at all ages,* and adolescence is simply one of them. Remember Genesis 2:24? "For this reason a man will leave his father and mother . . ." Adam and Eve were told that family changes would come as children grew up and moved out of the home. Adolescence is the beginning of that process. Believe it or not, I am more concerned when I do *not* see some moves toward independence in the lives of twelve to eighteen year olds.

We will be discussing typical developmental changes. Many of the things that you are seeing in your teen are typical, expected, and probably quite healthy. This does not mean, however, that teens do not need significant guidance during this challenging time. We must cultivate the ability to discern "normal" adolescence from development gone awry.

Secondly, the values that you have instilled in your child are still there and will resurface. This is no time for panic. Take hope in the Scripture that reassures us, "Train a child in the way he should go, and when he is old he will not turn from it." (Prov. 22:6) Thank God that all of your efforts at training and parenting are not lost. They have simply disappeared for a season, only to return later.

Finally, this is also a time for parents to review their own parenting styles. This will not be a passive time when you just "hold on and hope for the best." No, quite the opposite. You will be required to develop new skills and reexamine some old ones. The tools and techniques you learned for working with six-year-old Johnny will not work with fourteen-year-old John. Just when you may have been expecting parenting to get easier, your skills are pushed to the max.

Let's take a peek at some of the developmental changes that give rise to these "outrageous" behaviors. Perhaps we can help assuage some of your anxieties and lend some direction for the future. Remember the saying, "forewarned is forearmed"? That advice is especially important when dealing with teenagers.

"CALMNESS IS ALWAYS GODLIKE."

—*Ralph Waldo Emerson*

DEVELOPMENTAL CHANGES IN ADOLESCENCE

Parents of adolescence are often told not to take current problems personally. This is good advice, and you'll want to remind yourself of it again and again. After all, we spend many years trying to mold our children according to the values we believe in, attempting to shape them to be the best persons possible. It is no surprise, then, that at the first sign that our children are beginning to reject our values we panic. We often attempt, rather frantically, to regain control—a tactic that often backfires. Actually, those parents who are able to exert total control may end up regretting it in the end, when their children are unable to think for themselves or else undergo a more serious and harmful rebellion in years to come.

A brief reminder of some of the developmental and physiological changes brought on by adolescence may help allay some of your fears. Let us consider some of the changes occurring within adolescents.

Hormonal Changes. Adolescents and parents both sense that something different is happening. It is like a time bomb has exploded. As the adolescent's body changes physiologically, teens often experience moods and feelings more intensely and feel less control over them. This time bomb, called *puberty*, creates many changes. Outbursts of irritation and anger are common as adolescents learn about their moods and how to manage them. They are often confused about their bodily changes, and feel terribly self-conscious about them. They are embarrassed when the voice cracks, body hairs arrive unannounced, and limbs feel gangly and awkward. What may be worse is when some of these changes *do not happen* in their own bodies, but are happening to their peers. Teens are constantly comparing themselves with their friends to see if they measure up. To look too different would be unacceptable, and they'll go to any lengths to get the latest fashion so that they will fit in.

Peers are Number One. Children start out in this life completely dependent upon parents to care for them. This is natural, and a God-ordained pattern. But with the onslaught of adolescence comes a gradual shifting of dependency. You, as parents and family, will find yourself displaced by friends. Teens will prefer to be with their friends rather than be anywhere near the family. In fact, they may wail and moan if they have to spend much time with the family if their friends aren't there.

One of the most important developmental tasks for teens is to develop peer-relationship skills. It is a time to "practice" being who they will become. They will "test out" different aspects of their personality that you, as parents, may find particularly annoying. But all of this practice, which will probably include dating the opposite sex, is part of finding out who they are.

During this time the adolescent will push away physically as well as emotionally. This is a time when they may ask to be away from home more often. The phone may appear to be growing out of one of their ears. A second phone line may become a serious topic of conversation.

New Thinking Skills. You will quickly discover that your teen is developing a new ability to reason, and this will take the form of arguing with you. Again, not to be alarmed. They are testing their thinking and reasoning skills in the safest possible place: home.

As they test out these concepts of "fairness" and what is "right and wrong" and various aspects of their emerging morality, caution must be taken to not engage in too many verbal battles. They can outlast you in most verbal struggles, and the relationship usually suffers in the process. There is wisdom in the advice, "Choose your battles carefully."

"I THINK, THEREFORE I AM."

—*Rene Descartes*

Ambivalence about Responsibility. Issues about responsibility are sure to surface. While on the one hand teens will beg for greater freedoms and the responsibility attached to those freedoms, they are not yet mature enough to really handle complete freedom. They will make mistakes because they are still maturing. Your task as parents is to give them opportunities to practice responsibility by way of chores around the home and perhaps a job outside the home. However, you must be patient because they will likely be quite imperfect at accomplishing their responsibilities. They will have to learn from consequences the results of failing to live up to agreed upon responsibilities.

Self-Preoccupation. If parents were not able to rationalize away their teens' obsession with themselves, I think the situation could become intolerable. Adolescence is a time when teens focus on their own needs and desires to the exclusion of other family members. They seem to believe that the world revolves around them. This, of course, causes no end of conflicts within the family, where there must be at least a semblance of teamwork.

It is often this preoccupation with self that causes quarrels in the family. When the teen shows little regard for the well-being of others, family members often feel bitter toward the teen. It is no longer an issue simply between parent and child as the rest of the family enter the fray.

James aptly talks about the selfish motivations within the teen that lead to their contentious behavior. He says, "What causes fights and quarrels among you? Don't they come from your desires that battle within you? You want something but don't get it" (James 4:1).

A Push for Independence. Teenagers are desperate for more and more freedom. In fact, in my work with teens, they seem to rarely be satisfied with the amount of freedom they receive. They are constantly pushing for more. Parents mistakenly believe that if they give their teen a certain amount of freedom they will be happy. This is not likely to happen.

There is a natural tendency for teens to push away from their parents, and sometimes this pushing gets stormy. Sometimes it is the only way they know how to push away from the family. While they want greater freedom and want to prepare to live on their own without the restrictions of their parents, deep within there is also some trepidation about this move. Rarely are they able to give voice to these mixed feelings, so they call loudly for fewer limitations. They are in the process of making the normal break from family life to independent living, from childhood to adulthood.

A Search for Identity. Teenagers are desperate for a sense of identity. They will search for a group to which they may belong that will give them an opportunity to "try on" that identity. They may switch groups and friendships as they go on in this search. They may try out different dress styles as they search for what really expresses who they are. The thing for parents to remember is that they are in transition, and today's dress style or group affiliation may not be the same one they have two months from now.

To see your handsome son come home one day in ragged jeans, or a daughter's beautiful hair chopped off (apparently with a dull pair of scissors) can be a shocking thing. This is another sure sign that your teens are trying on different aspects of their personality. Be careful about overreacting because this will simply set up a power struggle that you do not want—or need—to engage in. In my opinion, many of these power struggles are needless. An example will illustrate what I am talking about.

When our oldest son entered adolescence, family life as we had known it came to an end. He made it clear that he was going to think differently than the stodgy ways of his parents, would dress differently, and was going to be his own person. This included baggy clothing, scruffy hair, and an earring. All of these strong declarations pushed every one of my buttons of propriety, and I was determined to win. Fortunately, however, this struggle was short-lived, as my wife came to the rescue with her wisdom. She again reminded me that in winning over some of these "trivial" issues I would lose our son's relationship. "Choose your battles carefully," she advised.

> "IDENTITY IS WHAT YOU CAN SAY
> YOU ARE ACCORDING TO WHAT
> THEY SAY YOU CAN BE."
>
> —*Jill Johnston*

Identity

WHEN BEHAVIOR BECOMES A CONCERN

You may be facing your own version of body-piercing, outrageous clothing changes, hair styles, and choice of activities. Any one of these issues is enough to give you a bad day, and perhaps even a bad week. They are enough to cause a significant power-struggle for weeks. How is one to decide which issues are important and which are trivial, which can cause permanent damage and which will pass soon?

There is a statement that I hear quite often from parents: "This is not normal behavior." Of course, sometimes they are right. The difficulty lies in differentiating normal from abnormal behavior. There is a wide spectrum of human behavior that we all consider normal. It is only as the behavior approaches certain limits that we consider it to be abnormal.

In addition to the question of normalcy, however, we want to ask ourselves if this behavior is in line with the values and morality that we are promoting in our family. Clearly there are many behaviors that fit in nicely with the culture around us but do not fit into the values we claim as a family. *We never need to give in to the pressure the teen may place on us to subscribe to cultural values.* Being clear about our values and differentiating them from that of popular culture is an important task that makes your family different from others. You have your own uniqueness that will help to guide you in these difficult decisions.

So, how do we decide when to intervene in some our of our teens' behaviors and choices? What are some indicators that the behavior has gone beyond normalcy and requires immediate attention?

Violation of Moral Principles. One of our first guides for determining if intervention is needed is when behavior violates our moral values. For an obvious example, if your adolescent decides to experiment with drugs, this would violate most parents' standards of proper care for their bodies. The Scriptures are clear about how we are to treat our bodies, and use and abuse of drugs or alcohol do not fit into that pattern.

Likewise, if your teen were involved with shoplifting or other forms of stealing, this would violate your values. Your prohibition of stealing may also apply to more subtle forms of the same behavior. For example, teens are notorious for "borrowing" things that do not belong to them. While they want their privacy respected rigidly, they often do not offer the same respect to others. And for many teens, cheating in school is seen as perfectly acceptable behavior, because "everybody does it."

Disrespect toward Others. It is critical that teens learn to treat others with respect. Depending on the teen, this may be a simple task or a difficult one. No matter how hard it is, teaching teens to respect their elders and others in authority is a building block of adult civil behavior.

It is, unfortunately, common for teens to treat their parents and other authority figures with disrespect. They seem to think that they can be abusive with their language, with no consequences or repercussions. When they were children they would not think of calling their parents a disrespectful name. Suddenly, as adolescents, their attitude toward authority has changed to such a radical extent that they may believe they owe no one respect. It should be understood, however, that parents must model respect. Parents who lose their temper and call their adolescent names is simply modeling the behavior they want extinguished.

Aggression. With hormones raging and moods on a wild pendulum, adolescents may let their tempers flare with increased regularity. Again, it is critical that youth learn that they cannot discharge anger anywhere or in any way they desire. The constraints of proper family and societal order come into play.

If there is a pattern of aggression where others consistently feel threatened, are threatened, or are actually hurt, immediate intervention is needed. This suggests that the teens are dealing with some very difficult emotions or that their behavior has become a way of being for them. If there are any indicators that your teen is intentionally harming others, whether physically or emotionally, this should cause immediate concern.

Disregarding Others' Boundaries. While it is certainly normal for adolescents to violate and "test" boundaries, again, this should not become a patterned way of living. An occasional crossing of the line is acceptable, while a consistent violation of others' boundaries can be a serious indicator of deeper problems.

If you sense that your teen lacks the ability to manage his or her behavior in such a way as to honor and respect boundaries and limits, professional help may be needed. However, it is imperative that the parent set clear limits for the adolescent. Parents often confuse the teen when they set a boundary and then change the rules. Excessive leniency causes significant problems as the teen does not know what behavior is really expected.

A word about unity between parents is in order. It is very easy for children to practice the manipulative tool of "dividing and conquering." When one parent is too strict and the other too lenient, teens know how to play one parent against the other. They know how to manipulate the parents for their own interests. Take care that you and your spouse are agreed about the rules and expectations in the home.

Lack of Remorse. It can be disheartening when your teen has done something wrong, and then seems so hardened so as to not feel any empathy or remorse for that behavior. When your teen has a limited ability to *feel remorse and take responsibility for wrong behavior,* there is a significant developmental problem.

Perhaps more common than a total lack of remorse is a cousin of this behavior: excuse-making. Teens are famous for being able to rationalize away their wrongdoing, blame it on others, or generally try to confound you so as to avoid any culpability. These "thinking errors" need attention and must be dealt with immediately.

Often teens appear to not care when really under their tough facade they feel badly for their behavior. If you seriously question their ability to feel others pain, or see the damage that they are causing others, this is a troubling sign.

Refusal to Accept Responsibility for Wrongdoing. It is quite common for teens to blame others for their problems. Yet, some time after the incident in question, they can usually see how they participated in or even caused the problem. If they totally refuse to take any ownership of the problem, or if there is a blatant pattern of blaming others, they may be heading for more serious problems. If they cannot accept that they have behaviors that need attention, then they will make no effort to correct them.

Pattern of Depression or Low Self-Esteem. There is, admittedly, a wide spectrum of behavior that should be considered normal. The issue here is the duration and intensity of these thoughts and moods. Clearly if the depression is sustained for more than a few days consistently, or if the moods are severe enough for the teen to begin to alter his or her behavior significantly, then a consultation may be in order. If the teen has any thoughts of suicide—and you should feel free to ask about your teen's feelings—the teen should be seen immediately by a professional.

Substance Abuse. Unfortunately, substance abuse is all too common, and its effects can mimic any of the above symptoms. It is quite possible that the symptoms you are seeing are really an effect of drug or alcohol use. If you question this at all, you should seek the advice of a professional in this field. It is unlikely that a teen will be honest about any substance use, and you may need the input of a professional to determine if there is a problem.

Societal Influences

Many ask what has caused this rapid increase in adolescent difficulties in the home. Let us briefly look at some of the societal influences in these family struggles, and then we will look into the life of a family currently in the throes of serious turmoil and ways they have found to grow through the challenges.

Family Instability. Perhaps the biggest change within the family structure over the past decade has been the incredible instability of the family. With the divorce rate hovering at 50 percent it is not uncommon for children to be raised in either single-parent families or stepfamilies. Although we are working harder than ever to understand the impact of these changes on the children involved, we do know that many of these changes have some detrimental effects on them.

Take the single-parent family, for instance. In many of these homes the single parent must find enough time to earn a living, care for the practical household needs, raise children, and meet their own social needs. Not surprisingly, this daunting task has been shown to be incredibly stressful. The children involved in these family situations often show more symptoms of stress than children from two-parent families, often leading to more aggression and frustration.

What effects are we seeing from the rise in stepfamilies? In this situation there are two different families living together as one, creating their own unique strains upon all family members. There are adjustments that need to be made, for which there has often been no preparation or instructions. There is often an inadequate amount of time in which to make the adjustments, leading to family turmoil and aggression. Stepfamily situations are fertile grounds for family conflict and division. (See **Your Pocket Therapist** Booklet on Stepfamilies.)

Another twentieth century phenomenon adding to instability is the mobile family. Not only are we not staying to live with our parents and grandparents in the supportive structure of the extended family, but we are not even living in the same state or town as our extended family. Isolated and left to cope with family struggles on their own, parents often feel the pressure of raising the family without the necessary help.

It has been said that the average adult will change jobs seven times, often creating several family moves. Consider the stress that it puts upon the children to make new friends in each of these new environments. This lack of stability adds additional stress to the family, and may overtax a weak family system.

Working Parents. Never before in our history have there been so many sets of working parents. Out of necessity, or simply the desire to get ahead financially and obtain all the benefits that prosperity offers, many homes have dual-income parents. What effect has this "latch-key" environment had on the children? Surely there have been numerous benefits when it comes to financial opportunities and the things that money can buy. But how has it added to family stress? How has it contributed to the possible weakening of the family structure?

The number-one complaint that I hear from dual-income families is exhaustion. Often both are working full work weeks, sometimes even different work hours. While they have more material benefits, in the form of a larger home and newer car, they complain of being tired and having less time to cultivate marital satisfaction and family enrichment.

Violence in Society. What effect has it had on the family to be bombarded daily—via news media, movies, and television programs—with unrelenting images of violence? Have we become desensitized to the violence? Do we barely turn our heads at the latest statistics suggesting that we are a society that is out of control?

Not that many years ago, the biggest problems in our schools had to do with children chewing gum in class and getting out of their seats without raising their hands. Today we are concerned with gangs, violence, teacher and student safety, and killings on campus. It has reached the point where we now have police on many campuses in our nation. What effect, do you suppose, does this have on our ability as parents to exert control over the behavior of our children?

Having considered these environmental and societal influences on our families, let us now take a closer look at a family who is in distress, feeling like they are literally coming apart at the seams.

> "FAMILIES ARE ABOUT LOVE
> OVERCOMING EMOTIONAL TORTURE."
>
> —*Matt Groening*

THE JACKSON FAMILY

I received a call from the Jacksons asking for an appointment immediately. They were in crisis. It seems that they had been having an inordinate amount of conflict with their son, Ben, over recent months, to the point where there had been some physical violence and much verbal conflict. They felt unprepared to deal with this kind of intense conflict, and it was pushing their family apart. The situation appeared to be urgent.

Carol Jackson asked who should come for their first appointment, though assuring me that Ben, their sixteen-year-old son, would probably not be willing to attend. I told her that I would like to see her and her husband, and Ben if he would be willing to attend. I encouraged her to attempt to convey to Ben that it would be helpful for him to attend, and that his point of view would be taken very seriously. I also told her to inform him that he could have a time alone with me if that would make a difference.

Carol called back the following day. Ben would not come with them, but would be willing, reluctantly, to come and see me alone, and I could see his parents without him as well. I agreed to this arrangement and set up times for both Ben and his parents.

The following week I saw Carol and Ron Jackson. They were a couple in their mid-forties and had two younger children, ages 12 and 10. It seems that the Jacksons saw themselves as a middle-class family with strong moral values and religious convictions. Carol worked as an elementary-school teacher while Ron worked at a paper manufacturing company as a sales representative. While Ron had a tendency to work long hours and had to spend some time on the road to do his job, they saw the family as tightly knit. They had had no significant family problems in the past, and their current difficulties were very difficult for them to handle. They could see their close family disintegrating before their eyes. They had come to me on the advice of their pastor.

I asked the Jacksons to tell me more about the exact nature of their problems, and the way that they were handling them.

It seems that Ben had been a very "normal" child who had no significant behavioral problems or developmental difficulties to speak of, though he did seem to acquire a few social problems as he became older. He was the quietest of their three children, but had seemed to compensate for any difficulties he had. His two younger sisters were more outgoing, and already had more friends than he, though this did not seem to bother him.

The Jacksons had always been pleased with their son, and he had always handled himself with good manners. The few friends that he always had seemed to like him, and he treated them well. They added that they had always encouraged Ben to participate in some kind of extra-curricular activity to ward off tendencies to withdraw. They wondered if this pattern of withdrawal could convey some underlying self-esteem issue, but decided it had to do with his innate temperament and was not any kind of deficiency.

I asked them about Ben's relationships with his sisters and themselves. They stated that his relationship with his sisters had always been somewhat combative, but especially in recent weeks. In fact, they felt that he had been outright cruel to them, for no apparent reason. They stated that he had been a distant child to his parents at times, but could also be very loving. He had a "tender heart." He was probably closer to his father, but had also had a close relationship with his mother. That was all up until about six months ago.

Since then, Ben began behaving differently. It was not a subtle change, they stated. It felt to them like it was an overnight shift in values and behavior. He began challenging everything his parents told him, and became increasingly angry and defiant with them. In fact, they remember Ben saying that he wanted to decide his own values, and that everything that they had taught him may no longer be his values. The Jacksons shared how much that simple statement had hurt them. It felt to them that he was rejecting everything they had tried hard to teach him over the years.

The Jacksons continued their story, saying that Ben also began to pick up some bad habits from his new friends at school. He had a flippant attitude toward many things. While he still wanted to go to school, good grades were now optional, not a necessity. He began to question anything that they said to him, and became quite argumentative. He wanted an explanation for all of their decisions, and if it did not turn out his way he would become very angry. There was a new level of moodiness to him, and they wondered at times if he were depressed. He told them that he was not, but they felt that he could not tolerate minor irritations the way that he had in the past.

Perhaps the hardest thing for the Jacksons to deal with was Ben's deception with them. He tested their limits, and then would lie to their faces about his activities. While they did not see any evidence of seriously bad behavior, they were not sure what he was really doing because he was not as open with them anymore, and was often deceptive. When caught with his deceptiveness he seemed remorseful, yet repeated his behavior again later. This pattern, they said, was creating a constant state of tension in the family.

I asked them about their expectations with Ben, and how they handled it when he violated their rules. They told me that they had negotiated a curfew with him of midnight on weekends, although that was revoked if he did not attend church the next morning. This system had not worked most of the time, although he kept promising that he would do better. He became angry when they revoked the agreement and told him that he could not go out on Saturday evenings. In regard to his other multiple violations, such as blatant deception, they would ground him for a week, with some effectiveness.

Ron said that one of the things that troubled him the most was Ben's new appearance. He had always taken pride in his children's appearance. Ben had decided that he no longer wanted to look like everyone else, and dressed in gaudy looking attire. He shopped at Goodwill stores, not for price savings, but for the particular look he was after. His hair hung down over his face. Any criticism of his son's dress would be certain to spark an eruption.

As the session neared its close we all agreed that Ben was going through some major changes, and that these were most difficult for them to tolerate. They wondered if these changes were normal and whether they were doing things the right way or were somehow making things worse. As the Jacksons sat there sharing their pain and tears, I supported their efforts to repair things, and the pain they had all been experiencing. I ended our time by telling them that they had done the right thing by seeking assistance from their pastor and now coming to see me. I knew that it took courage on their part to admit that things were out of control and to ask for help.

Meeting With Ben

Ben entered my office slowly and cautiously. While he assumed an air of self-confidence, I strongly suspected this to be a cover for the apprehension anyone would feel in those circumstances. He looked around at the different articles on my desk and coffee table and seemed to offer his nonverbal approval.

There was something about Ben that I immediately liked. He was not a hardened teen who was looking for ways to rob banks and take advantage of people. He still had a great deal of innocence left in him, though I do not think that his parents could see that. After several minutes of checking out me and my office he began to warm up a little. He was not about to offer much and made it clear that he did not think that going to a "shrink" was necessary. He wanted me to acknowledge his independence and not attempt to control him in any way. That was fine with me, and was exactly what I expected from him.

I asked nonthreatening questions at first. I simply wanted to develop a rapport with him and let him know that I was not going to psychoanalyze him, but simply wanted to help to make home life better for everyone. He wanted that too.

After a while I asked him what he wanted different from his family. He immediately shared his frustration about his younger sisters, feeling like they were always an intrusion into his life at a time when he wanted more privacy. He was also angry about his parents' attempts to "know everything" about his life, when he was "old enough" to make his own decisions. Their prying into his life really upset him, and he was not about to open up to them. He had strong convictions and needs when it came to privacy and a desire to begin making his own decisions, and perhaps even his own mistakes.

After he had vented his frustration we prepared to end our time together. He agreed that he would meet again with me, but made no commitment to come for any set length of time. I felt good about our time together because Ben had shared some of his pain and wanted things to be different at home. I thought that he may be willing, in time, to put some effort into negotiating with his parents for some things which would bring relief to all.

Family Therapy

As the weeks went by I met with both Ben and his parents separately, and then finally we had some conjoint sessions. It became clear fairly quickly that Ben was not a "rebellious child," but rather a young man who was seeking his own identity. This is a major task of teenagers, and often forgotten by parents. He sought his identity by challenging their beliefs, wearing different clothes, and even talking in different ways. He did not want to be just like them. As with most change, the pendulum went quite a ways off to one direction, but I assured the Jacksons that it would find a middle ground.

The family therapy established some expectations for Ben's parents, encouraging them to give him the privacy he needed and the room to make mistakes. Ben was asked to make some changes as well. He was expected to treat his parents with respect and abide by their decisions even if they did not meet his desired outcomes. They, in turn, would work at really listening to his point of view, and not assume that he was wrong just because he looked at things differently than they did.

Perhaps the most important thing that happened in the few months that the Jacksons allowed me into their lives was a new level of respect for one another. The walls of anger began to break down and listening began to happen. They learned how to avoid hot arguments and come back to an issue when things had cooled.

Things would never be perfect between them. Ben was just not "their child" anymore but was his own person, with different values and beliefs. He may or may not make some of the choices that they would make or want him to make. They had to practice "letting go." Ben had to learn that if he violated their boundaries there would be agreed-upon consequences. They had developed better ways of asking for what they needed, and better ways of expressing anger toward one another. Each had a clearer understanding of the expectations of the other.

What Adolescents Wish Parents Understood about Them

While we often complain about the behavior of adolescents, seldom do we really sit down and listen to what they have to say. Most teens are quite willing to be candid with us as we search for answers to the problems. It seems appropriate to hear from the adolescents themselves about what they would like from adults that would be helpful to them. The following are some of the requests that they make repeatedly of adults. See if you fall into any of the patterns.

Treat Me with Respect! As parents become more embittered with their children it becomes harder to treat them with respect, especially when the children are treating them disrespectfully. The children feel this underlying animosity and resent it. They often say, "I'll act just the way they expect me to act." It is critical to remember to treat your adolescent with kindness and dignity even if your feelings are to the contrary. Using respect often is an anger defuser and sets a positive tone on which to build.

Respect My Privacy! You will often notice greater degrees of privacy needs by your adolescent. This may be viewed, and felt, as "secrecy," but more often it is their desire to be their own persons. This seems to require more space and a distancing from the boundaries of the family. It is only when there seems to be a morbid withdrawal from the world that there needs to be concern.

Listen to My Opinions! Teenagers hate decisions being made about them without their input. They usually have strong feelings and opinions about situations and are ready to share those opinions. When they sense an indifference to their opinions, this feels like profound disrespect to them. It does wonders to include them in decision-making processes, especially when it concerns them.

Don't Lecture Me! Teenagers hate being lectured to. Even though parents often feel like they are not "getting it," it may be more effective to simply set the consequences and leave it at that. It's tough to see your children going through painful experiences that they could have avoided, but prolonged discussions can create bitterness and seldom lead to greater learning.

Treat Me Like an Adult! While there may be ambivalence about how much responsibility teens want to take on, make no mistake that they desire to be talked to, and treated, like adults. Even when their behavior does not match adult behavior, try treating them in an adult, respectful manner and notice the improved results. They have begun to view themselves as adults, and would like that perspective mirrored by their parents.

"COURAGE IS RESISTANCE TO FEAR,

MASTERY OF FEAR—

NOT ABSENCE OF FEAR."

—*Mark Twain*

Courage

A Final Challenge to Parents

While parenting adolescents is a challenge, I'm afraid that it has been described by too many as an impossible task. I wonder if we set ourselves up for unneeded difficulties when we label all adolescents as "rebellious" or "brain damaged." Is it possible that parenting adolescents can also be very enjoyable, and perhaps challenging to us in a positive way?

When parents of adolescents are counseled to fasten their seatbelts for the ride of their lives it creates a mindset of passivity and hopelessness. It is critical that parents *not be passive, or victims,* but rather approach this time in family life courageously to learn more about their own styles of parenting and weaknesses within themselves that cry out to be strengthened. Let's consider some of the challenges that must be faced by parents of adolescents. By labeling them as challenges, by the way, I am attempting to avoid casting the tasks in a negative light. Adolescence is simply a developmental phase with its unique aspects, not unlike the inherent joys and struggles of other phases of childhood. So what are the challenges for parents?

The Challenge of Admiration

Everyone, especially adolescents, have a need to be appreciated and admired. You will never hear a teen tell you that they need to be admired, but you can trust that it is there. They not only need to be admired, but *they need to be told that they are appreciated and admired.* This means recognizing and affirming the character traits that you appreciate in them. You know what they are. They have been a part of your child from the beginning.

The obvious difficulty with this assignment is that you may be struggling with even liking them at this moment, let alone appreciating them. Their behavior over a period of time may have brought feelings of resentment between you and your teens. The task, then, is twofold. It requires that you manage your feelings of frustration toward them, while also remembering what you love and admire about them—and telling them.

While teens may never ask for admiration, remember that their identity is still very fragile at this point. They may never let on that they are struggling, but you can be sure that there are battles taking place every day within your teen. Just as adults hunger for recognition and appreciation, your teen longs to be appreciated as well. Take care to compartmentalize the times of difficulty and frustration to allow the times of joy and laughter to be a strong and enduring aspect of the relationship.

THE CHALLENGE OF MATURITY

It is somewhat surprising to see the regularity with which parents of adolescents resort to the same behavior that they dislike in their children. We scold our teens for their use of foul language, but model it ourselves when angry. We hate their verbal maneuvers to engage us in debate, yet we so easily fall into that same pattern of arguing with them. We must remember that it takes two to continue an argument.

I remember all too well the stormy years of two adolescents in our home. Nearly everything they did pushed one or more of my buttons. If it was not their tone of voice, it was their "attitude." If not their attitude, it was their lack of self-discipline. Unfortunately, at times I did not handle these situations with calmness and maturity, but rather with indignance and anger. This, of course, only served to fuel the fire.

My wife had her turn in the hopper as well. At times she lost her cool and caught herself in a verbal tirade that did not help the situation at all. We vowed to "help one another"—in sort of a tag-team effort—if we began to "lose it." I applaud those of you who are single parents for attempting the feat of raising an adolescent on your own.

So, in all of the swirling emotional and hormonal turmoil, our challenge is to keep our heads clear and remember where we are going. Remember that it is our task to keep the ship level, so to speak, and keep the family pointed in the right direction. We must model maturity for them.

REVIEW OUR VALUES

Adolescence is a great opportunity for parents to review what they believe on a variety of issues. Yes, you read *opportunity!* If you can create an attitude of opportunity, seeing the challenges inherent in this season of life, you will make it through much more easily.

Many issues will rise during this time. In fact, so many issues will bubble to the surface that you will find yourself in a state of confusion more often than you would like. You will probably find yourself seeking out other parents in similar situations to compare notes. I heartily recommend that you do that.

One issue up for review will be the decision about how strict or lenient you will be. You were raised with a certain disciplinary style, and it is common to perpetuate those patterns in your own family. "That's how I was raised, and it worked for me," is a common refrain. But your spouse was undoubtedly raised somewhat differently, and you will need to discuss which methods work for both of you. The art of compromise may come into play here. Remember that all the time you are working out your particular approach to discipline your adolescent will be moving forward with his or her own agenda.

You will also need to determine how you feel about letting your teens make their own mistakes as opposed to protecting them. There are different schools of thought on this issue and no "right" answer. I will not offer any firm opinion in any of these areas, as I believe that these are personal values that you must clarify for yourself.

Of course you will also need to determine, preferably ahead of time, how you feel about the practical aspects of raising a teen. When will you let them date, and under what circumstances? When will you let them drive, and will you be paying auto insurance for them? Will you be requiring them to attend church and youth group, or will they be allowed to decide those things for themselves?

The list goes on and on. The important thing is that you become as clear as possible ahead of time so that you can offer your teens clear direction with firm boundaries. Remember that they will probably challenge you at every turn, so you must have a ready answer. Your answer need not hold up to the scrutiny of the Supreme Court, however. This is your home and you are promoting your values. That is what makes your family unique. You are not exactly like the Joneses down the street.

THE CHALLENGE OF MAINTAINING YOUR OWN LIFE

In the midst of the tumultuous teen years it can be easy to lose your own life. If you are not careful, your entire focus will be on raising your teen. Please do not misunderstand. Our teens need us more than ever at this stage in their development. Yet, at the same time, they will soon be gone and your marriage must remain robust and alive.

I have, unfortunately, seen too many couples who squabbled over how to raise their children and forgot that they would be sitting alone across the dining room table from one another in a few short years. There would be no distractions to keep them from looking closely at the way they had become accustomed to interacting with one another. In too many instances this turned out to be a real crisis for them. It could have been averted if they had remembered that their challenges with their teen, and perhaps other children, was a temporary job, while maintaining a healthy marriage was a lifelong commitment.

Not only must you maintain your marriage, but you must maintain your life. They should not be one and the same. You are an individual apart from your relationship to your spouse. Have you fallen into the trap of letting your passions slip to the side? Have you given up too many of your hobbies to care for the kids? Take care of yourself and remember that when the kids are gone you will be left to fill the empty spaces.

Summary

Raising an adolescent can be like entering a foreign country—not knowing the language, with a dose of hostility added. It is hard to know what to expect and what is coming next. Most of what you will be facing will be quite "normal" and, fortunately, it won't last forever. "This too shall pass." We have noted that it will also be important to capture the joys of parenting a teen in addition to the challenges.

It is possible, though difficult, to use this time for self-growth as well. Try to reframe your perspective, seeing this phase of parenting as another opportunity. See if you can learn more about yourself and your teenager throughout this process. Try to view this stage as a challenge, finding creative ways to overcome obstacles. Keep a positive outlook, and know that you can grow closer to your teen in the process.

Finally, hold on to the wisdom that tells us that our children will return to the values that they have been taught throughout their lives, even if they cast them off for a season.

FOR FURTHER READING:

1. Dobson, James. Preparing for Adolescence. Colorado Springs: Focus on the Family, 1995.

2. Ginott, Haim. Between Parent and Teenager. New York: The Macmillan Company, 1969.

3. Gordon, Thomas. Parent Effectiveness Training. New American Library, 1975.

4. Huggins, Kevin. Parenting Adolescents. Colorado Springs: The Navigators, 1989.

5. Ziglar, Zig. Raising Positive Kids in a Negative World. Nashville: Thomas Nelson Publishers, 1985.